# The Enormous Watermelon

## by Alison Hawes
## illustrated by Elba Rodriguez

CAMBRIDGE
UNIVERSITY PRESS

UCL
Institute of Education

Ravi and his mum picked
lots of mangoes and
lots of oranges.

They picked
an **enormous** watermelon,
too.

Mum and Ravi could carry the mangoes and oranges.

But they couldn't carry the **enormous** watermelon, too!

Then Ravi saw
the wheelbarrow.

'I know what I can do!'
he said.

Ravi carried the watermelon in the wheelbarrow.

'Clever Ravi!' said Mum.

Ravi and his mum sold
lots of mangoes and
lots of oranges.

But they didn't sell
the **enormous** watermelon.

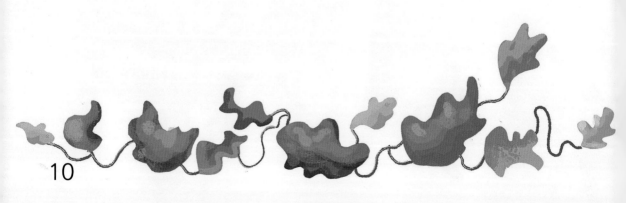

Then Mum saw the knife.

'I know what I can do!'
she said.

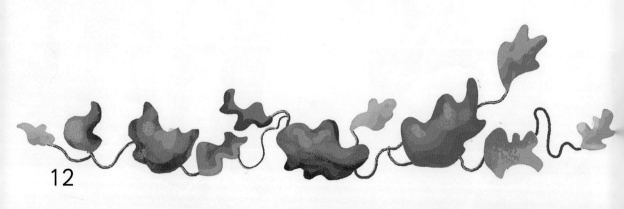

Mum cut the watermelon
with the knife.

They sold lots and lots
of watermelon.

Clever Mum!

# The Enormous Watermelon 🍉 Alison Hawes

Teaching notes written by Sue Bodman and Glen Franklin

## Using this book

### Developing reading comprehension

This story shows Mum and Ravi solving a problem. The story parallels other familiar and traditional tales about fruit or vegetables that grow larger than the norm and are hard to harvest.

### Grammar and sentence structure

- Repetition of phrases and a recurring theme support the reading.
- Text features such as bold text and punctuation support phrased and expressive reading.

### Word meaning and spelling

- Opportunity to rehearse and recognise known words in context.
- Longer words such as 'watermelon' and 'wheelbarrow' can be used to demonstrate location of known items which can be used to solve unfamiliar words.

### Curriculum links

*Maths* - The story lends itself to mathematics activities on division and fractions. How many people could buy a slice of watermelon if it was cut in different ways?

*Citizenship* - Explore the theme of sharing and how everyone was able to have a piece of the melon. Omar Can Help (Yellow band) also has the theme of sharing.

## Learning outcomes

Children can:

- solve simple words by blending phonemes from left to right and check for meaning, correct syntax i.e. does it make sense and sound right?
- locate and read high frequency words
- show an understanding of the elements of stories

- start to read in a more phrased manner while maintaining track of the print.

## A guided reading lesson

### Book Introduction

Give each child a book and read the title to them.

### *Orientation*

Check that all the children know what a watermelon is and share some experiences of eating them, for example, how refreshing they are, what to do with the pips. Ensure children understand the word 'enormous'.

Give a brief overview of the book, using the verb in the same form as it is in text.

*This is a book about Ravi and his Mum. They picked lots of fruit and are taking it all to market to sell. They had an enormous watermelon. It was too big to carry. But Ravi was clever. Shall we find out what he did?*

### *Preparation*

Pages 2 and 3: Provide some of the vocabulary on the page in a natural way: *Here's Ravi and his Mum. They picked lots of mangoes and lots of oranges to take to market.*

Draw attention to the watermelon: *'Look! Here's the watermelon. Oh, it is enormous, isn't it? Find the word 'enormous' on the page. What do you notice? Yes, it's in bold print. Remember that means we can say it loudly. Practise reading the line with expression on the word 'enormous'.*

*It was such a big watermelon that Mum and Ravi couldn't carry it! What could they do?* Listen to the children's suggestions.

Page 4: Ravi has a wheelbarrow. Take this opportunity to explore this compound word. Clap the syllables of 'wheel' and 'barrow'. Have the children frame the two parts of the word with their fingers. *You can do the*